The Heavy Hippo

Ruth Wong

Illustrated by Chantal Stewart

We went to the science museum.
My friend Annie came, too.
We had fun in the animal section.

Science Museum

3

We saw a picture of a baby giraffe.

"Look, Dad!" I said. "You are as tall as that giraffe."

"We are both six feet tall, and it's only a baby!" laughed Dad.

17
16
15
14
13
12
11
10
9
8
7
6
5
4
3
2
1
feet

5

We saw a picture of a condor.

"Wow! Look at how wide
its wings are!" said Annie.

"They are wider than my arms,"
I said.

4

9 10
feet

We saw a picture of a kangaroo.

"A kangaroo can jump 25 feet!" said Mom.

"That's a long way!" said Annie.
"I can only jump three feet."

25 24 23 22 21 20 15

8

9

We saw a picture of a cheetah.

"Can I run as fast as a cheetah?" I asked.

"No," laughed Dad. "A cheetah can run
70 miles an hour!"

"Everything is faster, taller, or bigger than we are,"
I said.

Cheetahs can run up to 70 miles an hour.

Your speed 4 mph

11

We saw a picture of a hippopotamus.

"The hippo weighs more than both of us!" I said.

Hippo's weight: 4000 pounds

Your weight in pounds

0   4000

"Let's see if all of us would be as heavy as a hippo," said Mom.

Hippo's weight: 40

"The hippo still weighs more than all of us!"
we laughed.

Some other people were watching us.

"We'll help," they said.

Hippo's weight: 4000 poun

14

Your weight in pounds

0   4000

They all got on the scales with us.

"Now we are as heavy as a hippo!"
I said.

Hippo's weight: 4000 pounds

Your weight in pounds

0   4000